Music processed by Sambo Music Engraving Co
Printed in England

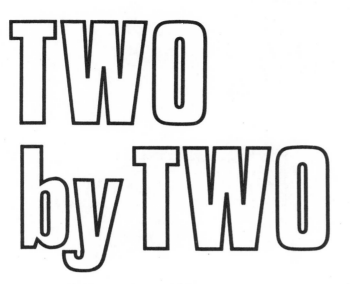

Two by Two

Mixed-ability duets for clarinet

Duette für Klarinetten von unterschiedlichem Schwierigkeitsgrad

Selected and edited by
PAUL HARRIS

CONTENTS . INHALT

FABER *ff* MUSIC

1 Overture

Paul Harris

2 Andante

Friedrich Berr
(1794–1838)

4

3 Allegretto

Xavier Lefèvre
(1763–1829)

4 Minuet

Henry Lazarus
(1815–1895)

5 Grasshopper

Paul Harris

6   Sloth

Paul Harris

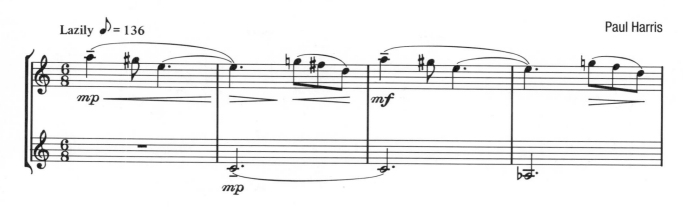

7 Two pieces from K487

I

Wolfgang Amadeus Mozart
(1756–1791)

II

8 Rondo

Xavier Lefèvre
(1763–1829)

9 Andante

Henry Lazarus
(1815–1895)

10 Canzonetta and Tarantella

Canzonetta

Nikolay Rimsky-Korsakov
(1844–1908)

Tarantella

Nikolay Rimsky-Korsakov
(1844–1908)

11 Waltz

Friedrich Berr
(1794–1838)

Mouvement de Valse ♩ = 132

12 Romance

Hyacinthe Klosé
(1808–1880)

13 Galumphing

Paul Harris

14 Polonaise

Johann Vanhal
(1739–1813)

15 Polonaise

Henry Lazarus
(1815–1895)

* ⌢ last time

16 Pastorale

Ludwig Weidemann
(1856–1918)

17 Scherzo

Robert Keitzer
(fl. late 19th century)

18 Silent Movie

Paul Harris

19 Non più Andrai

Wolfgang Amadeus Mozart
(1756–1791)

20 Toccata

Paul Harris